A REPORT FROM THE BORDER

Books by Anne Stevenson

POETRY

Living in America (Generation Press,
    University of Michigan, USA, 1965)
Reversals (Wesleyan University Press, USA, 1969)
Travelling Behind Glass: Selected Poems 1963-1973
    (Oxford University Press, 1974)
Correspondences, a Family History in Letters
    (Oxford University Press, 1974)
Enough of Green (Oxford University Press, 1977)
Sonnets for Five Seasons (Five Seasons Press, 1979)
Minute by Glass Minute (Oxford University Press, 1982)
A Legacy (Taxvs Press, 1983)
The Fiction Makers (Oxford University Press, 1985)
Wintertime (MidNAG, 1986)
Selected Poems 1956-1986 (Oxford University Press, 1987)
The Other House (Oxford University Press, 1990)
Four and a Half Dancing Men (Oxford University Press, 1993)
The Collected Poems 1955-1995
    (Oxford University Press, 1996; Bloodaxe Books, 2000)
Granny Scarecrow (Bloodaxe Books, 2000)
A Report from the Border (Bloodaxe Books, 2003)

LITERARY CRITICISM & BIOGRAPHY

Elizabeth Bishop (Twayne, USA, 1966)
Bitter Fame: A Life of Sylvia Plath
    (Viking, 1989; Houghton Mifflin, USA, 1989)
Between the Iceberg and the Ship: Selected Essays
    (University of Michigan Press, 1998)
Five Looks at Elizabeth Bishop
    (Bellew/Agenda Editions, 1998)

ANNE STEVENSON

A Report from the Border

NEW & RESCUED POEMS

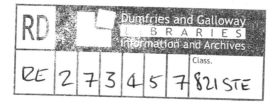

BLOODAXE BOOKS

Copyright © Anne Stevenson 2003

ISBN: 1 85224 616 2

First published 2003 by
Bloodaxe Books Ltd,
Highgreen,
Tarset,
Northumberland NE48 1RP.

www.bloodaxebooks.com
For further information about Bloodaxe titles
please visit our website or write to
the above address for a catalogue.

Bloodaxe Books Ltd acknowledges
the financial assistance of Northern Arts.

Cover printing by J. Thomson Colour Printers Ltd, Glasgow.

Printed in Great Britain by
Cromwell Press Ltd, Trowbridge, Wiltshire.

*In gratitude, to the friends who have
helped write these poems over the years*

Acknowledgements

Acknowledgements are due to the editors of the following publications where some of the poems or earlier versions of them first appeared: *Critical Survey*, *The Dark Horse*, *The Hudson Review*, *Literary Imagination* (USA), *London Magazine*, *Michigan Quarterly Review*, *New Writing 10* (Picador, 2001), *Other Poetry*, *Poetry Kanto 2002* (Japan), *Planet*, *PN Review*, *Poetry Review*, *Stand*, *Thumbscrew* and *The Times Literary Supplement*.

'The Wind, the Sun and the Moon' was published by Clutag Press, Oxford, in 2001. 'Washing My Hair' first appeared in *Wading through Deep Water*, published by The Parkinson's Society, 2001. 'Under Moefre' first appeared under the title 'At Bod-Loes-y-Gad' in a festschrift for Arnold Rattenbury, *To Arnold with Love* (Shoestring Press, 2001).

Fifteen of the new poems in *A Report from the Border* were earlier published in a pamphlet, *Hearing with My Fingers* (Thumbscrew Press, 2002). *A Report from the Border* also includes new versions of several poems "rescued" from previously published books. Early versions of 'Haunted' and 'Green Mountain, Black Mountain' appeared in *Minute by Glass Minute* (Oxford University Press, 1982). 'The Mass, The Media, The Market' and 'Branch Line' first appeared in *The Other House* (Oxford University Press, 1990). 'A Tourist Guide to the Fens' (then titled 'Level Cambridgeshire') and 'May Bluebells, Coed Aber Artro' were earlier published in *Four and a Half Dancing Men* (Oxford University Press, 1993). An earlier version of 'The Unaccommodated' appeared in *Collected Poems 1955-1995* (Oxford University Press, 1996; Bloodaxe Books, 2000). 'Why Take Agaist Mythology', parts I and 2, are revised from versions printed in *Granny Scarecrow* (Bloodaxe Books, 2000).

The writing of this book was assisted by a Northern Rock Foundation Writer Award for 2002-04, and thanks are due to all concerned.

Contents

Who's Joking with the Photographer?
(Photographs of myself approaching seventy)

(for Ernestine Ruben)

Not my final face, a map of how to get there.
Seven ages, seven irreversible layers, each
subtler and more supple than a snake's skin.
Nobody looks surprised when we slough off one
and begin to inhabit another.
Do we exchange them whole in our sleep, or
are they washed away in pieces, cheek by brow by chin,
in the steady abrasions of the solar shower?
Draw first breath, and time turns on its taps.
No wonder the newborn's tiny face crinkles and cries:
chill, then a sharp collision with light,
the mouth's desperation for the foreign nipple,
all the uses of eyes, ears, hands still to be learned
before the self pulls away in its skin-tight sphere
to endure on its own the tectonic geology of childhood.

Imagine in space-time irretrievable mothers viewing
the pensioners their babies have become.
'Well, that's life, nothing we can do about it now.'
They don't love us as much as they did, and
why should they? We have replaced them. Just as we're
being replaced by big sassy kids in school blazers.
Meanwhile, Federal Express has delivered my sixth face –
grandmother's, scraps of me grafted to her bones.
I don't believe it. Who made this mess,
this developer's sprawl of roads that can't be retaken,
high tension wires that run dangerously under the skin?
What is it the sceptical eyes are saying to the twisted lips:
ambition is a cliché, beauty a banality? In any case,
this face has given them up – old friends whose obituaries
it reads in the mirror with scarcely a regret.

So, who's joking with the photographer?
And what did she think she was doing,
taking pictures of the impossible? Was a radioscope
attached to her lens? Something teasing under the skull
has infiltrated the surface, something you can't see
until you look away, then it shoots out and tickles you.
You could call it soul or spirit, but that would be serious.
Look for a word that mixes affection with insurrection,
frivolity, child's play, rude curiosity,
a willingness to lift the seventh veil and welcome Yorick.
That's partly what the photo says. The rest is private,
guilt that rouses memory at four in the morning,
truths such as Hamlet used, torturing his mother,
all the dark half-tones of the sensuous unsayable
finding a whole woman there, in her one face.

The Writer in the Corner
Remembering Paul Winstanley

After long dying, short death.
One snip of the scissors,
One scoop of the palette knife,
The most ordinary nothing in the world,
That's the end of life.

Breathing still, still telling the story,
Wanting to believe there *is* a story,
They pour fresh flowers into the pit
Just before the bulldozer's
Earthen canopy slides over it.

How beautifully the church bells sing
To the crowd in black.
The widow lifts embroidered linen
To her kohl-rimmed eyes.
The canopy won't roll back.

There. They have dispersed.
The priest pays a visit to the toilet
Before he slips into his sky-blue Toyota.
A spray of gravel. He's off to celebrate
The bright day, the pure relief of it.

The upset cemetery, too, seems relieved
Now the bulldozer has understood it.
The driver and his mate light up,
Climb down, begin by habit
To decorate the ugly earth with wreathes.

They take no notice of the unshaved man,
Bald as the Sahara, dressed for youth
But long past it, scribbling in microscopic hand,
'What we live is the story,
What we write has to be the truth.'

Washing My Hair

Contending against a restless shower-head,
    I lather my own.
The hot tap, without a mind, decides
    to scald me;
The cold, without a will, would rather
    freeze me.
Turning them to suit me is an act of flesh
    I know as mine.
Here I am: scalp, neck, back, breasts,
    armpits, spine,
Parts I've long been part of, never
    treasured much,
Since I absorb them not *by* touch, more
    because of touch.
It's my mind, with its hoard of horribles,
    that's me.
Or is it really? I fantasise it bodiless,
    set free:
No bones, no skin, no hair, no nerves,
    just memory,
Untouchable, unwashable, and not, I guess,
    my own.
Still, none will know me better when I'm
    words on stone
Than I, these creased familiar hands
    and clumsy feet.
My soul, how will I recognise you
    if we meet?

Portrait of the Artist
in an Orthopaedic Halo Crowned with Flowers

She lives next door to dying
In a shack of bones,
A gorgeous spirit furnishing
That worst of homes.

A votive flame, she celebrates
The air she burns.
A flowering halo subjugates
Her crown of thorns.

Her eyes – amontillado
In the brimming glass –
Look straight into the Angel's.
But he will not pass.

Red Hot Sex

Miranda hoists her lips in a grimace.
Her arms are two peeled twigs, her ankles curl.
That dark soft hair and narrow porcelain face?
A sketch, a spoiled first draft of a pretty girl.

She's friendly with Fred, whose electronic chair
(State of the art for men who can't stand up)
Glides around hers, not touching anywhere.
He's spread into his, an egg (soft-boiled) in a cup,

So cheerfully disposed he makes a joke of that.
He's been in a chair since childhood. Awful burden.
Parents worn out in their eighties. Misses his cat.
A brother, whose wife can't cope, talks of a Home.

Here, he's neither home nor in a Home.
Laughing, he makes Miranda laugh. And me.
A heap among heaps, I glance around the room,
Our island of wheelers in a walking sea.

Thanks to the cash of a caring modern state,
We've space and food. It's institution-dreary,
But okay. When strong enough, I paint.
My helpers set me up in the conservatory,

Paint book, water glass, tray, plates of gouache.
Don't laugh when I tell you, all I paint is flowers.
As long as my Minnie Mouse paw can grip the brush
I forget my melting bones – for those few hours.

And once I can't paint? Never think of it.
No, not true, I do. I look around.
The TV's always on, and there they sit,
So many white-faced zombies. Gets you down.

What can you do? Your mind is seared with pain.
The worse your body, the more it seems to fill
Each tortured fold and cranny of your brain.
I haven't given up yet. I never will.

I pity Pete, for one, and sullen Clive
(Miranda hates it when they stare at her)
Who, half the time, don't seem to be alive.
No jokes, no books, no smirking at the paper,

Unless you count that section of *The Sun*
Stuffed in a plastic sack outside the lockers.
Red Hot Sex. Apologetic porn.
If the cover lovers hadn't both been starkers

They could have stepped right out of the TV.
She might have looked as sexy, selling weather.
And what's he fondling? His own vanity!
I wonder if they'd even met each other

Before they posed? Do actors, acting sex,
Feel anything but numb from the neck up?
$X + Y = Zero$. Solve for X.
Oh, thinking's hopeless! So I paint a tulip.

That lipstick red corolla is a show,
A lure, a pit where unsheathed pizzle-anthers
Practise the only sexy act they know;
Or mock-perform it – chancers playing nature's

Bingo, mixing the useless with the worthless,
Setting the lifewheel spinning, with no aim.
That's Mother Nature for you! I'm an artist.
Choosing to paint, I'm chosen. That's *my* game.

Passing Her House

(i.m. Nerys Johnson)

The house she nested in
became her,
unfurled around her
like a summer tree.
You can't pass by
that much desired but
costly new conservatory
without imagining she
still presides there,
tortured for hours
in her sadistic wheelchair,
but working quietly
among her pots and jars,
as if her brush were
walking through,
not painting flowers.

Was there some pheromone
her need unconsciously
released that drew
the needy to her? Who
came to care stayed
to be cared for. In Durham
she was queen-
creator of the hive's
heart, collector of humour's
nectar, conjurer
of sunlight out of gloom.
Her tools of rule
by telephone
were other people's lives;
they loved her for
not leaving them alone.

Those ziggurats of red
defiant shoes,
that dyed bright copper hair.
She laid her champagne tastes
for piquant news,
for waterlight and strawberries,
for art that makes necessity
its gesso, love that make
necessity its pleasure
over the private badlands
of her agonies.
How long, carissima,
before the house you were
forgets you?
Before I pass
forgetting to remember?

Passifloraceae

(i.m. Gordon Brown)

And then Gordon was so beautiful,
    not what we usually say of men;
Of him we do. Didn't everyone admire
    that glimmer of elusiveness
Shining through? Poetry's guardian angel,
    spirit of the Tower,
But ordinary, too. Cry, now, for the indefinable
    loneliness of fact.
There is always a reason to refuse reason,
    then choose to act.
The gorgeous corolla of the passion flower
    huddled in its sack
Chooses or doesn't choose a minute or an hour
    to unclench, fold back,
Reveal to its secret sharers the marvel
    of a story,
Esoteric and erect amid wild, predictable
    filaments of glory.

Gordon Brown, a much loved friend and poet, drowned himself in March
2000. For many people in Newcastle and Durham he represented the spirit of
Morden Tower where he initiated and arranged poetry readings over many
years.

A Marriage

When my mother knew why her treatment wasn't working,
She said to my father, trying not to detonate her news,
'Steve, you must marry again. When I'm gone, who's going
To tell you to put your trousers on before your shoes?'

My father opened his mouth to – couldn't – refuse.
Instead, he threw her a look; a man just shot
Gazing at the arm or leg he was about to lose.
His cigarette burned him, but he didn't stub it out.

Later, on the porch, alive in the dark together,
How solid the house must have felt, how sanely familiar
The street-lit leaves, their shadows patterning the street.
The house is still there. The elms and the people, not.

It was now, and it never was now. Like every experience
Of being entirely here, yet really not being.
They couldn't imagine the future that I am seeing,
For all his philosophy and all her common sense.

Haunted

It's not when you walk through my sleep
That I'm haunted most.
I am also alive where you were.
And my own ghost.

Hearing with My Fingers

A house with a six-foot rosewood piano, too grand
to get out the door? *You buy it, I'll play it!*
So now, as in my childhood, the living-room
has become the piano room, exercising,
like a sun, irresistible powers of gravitation.
How to walk past and not be dragged to keys
that free at a touch the souls of the composers?
The piano itself is soul-shaped. Like lovers,
our baby grands lay deep in each other's curves;
players locked eyes across the Yin and Yang of them,
fingering delight in a marriage of true sounds.

How would a living-room live without pianos,
I used to wonder, beginning my before-breakfast
two-hour stint at the Steinway, the Mason & Hamlin
dozing in its dotage. Scales, arpeggios,
Czerny or cheery Scarlatti, progressing through Bach
(stirrings in the kitchen, waftings of coffee and bacon)
to *Scenes from Childhood* that my hands, to my head's
amazement, still remember after forty years' neglect.

If I fancied myself an object of fate's attention,
I'd take for punishment the fog blinding my ears.
What was I doing those waste, egotistical years
when I snatched what I heard and never told the piano?
I wanted a contract with love. I wanted the words!
And now, apparently, my fingers have forgiven me.
Wordless as right and left, as right and wrong,
drained of ambition, gullied with veiny skin,
they want to go back and teach my eyes to listen,
my heart to see...the shape of a Greek amphora,
plum-blossom after Hiroshima, harmony-seeds
growing from staves my clumsy fingers read.

At the Grave of Ezra Pound

*Venice is an excellent place to come to from
Crawfordsville, Indiana.*
(Pavannes and Divagations)

Cimmerian? Anyway, a swart day.
Its silence immense, unfinished.
The leaden water pleated itself
As our boat drew close to the quay.

We passed through the aisle of bambini,
(White stones with coloured photographs,
Flowers in tender urns,
The pebbles washed, the graves shut and tidy)

And found the poet from Crawfordsville
In a dank, shady plot,
EZRA POUND, drilled into lichened rock.
Readable but not believable.

No *sylva nympharum* shone
Around him, tremulously clear.
No goddess of fair knees, no cave of Nerea,
No marble-leaved 'pleached arbour of stone'.

Olga alone, faithful and morose,
Shared his bracket of sour undergrowth
Where someone had knelt to plant the myrtle
Covering them both.

Whatever he might be writing
Wrathfully against our age
Moulders unheard, unwanted
On that tangled page.

Aletha, goddess of sea-farers, defend him.
'He fished by obstinate isles.'
In the gloom, what further betrayals
Gather the dark against him?

Skin Deep

Fashion is about eventually being naked.
VIVIENNE WESTWOOD

What a strange animal that has to get dressed
every morning!
Born with the free gift of a skin,
using it mainly to lie down in;
to bathe, to bask in the sun, to beget
in a snug, pungent, soft-sided, creaturely outfit,
love in it, sleep in it, die in it,
but until then
obsessively live with it
under that pesky Damoclesian ur-question,
what on earth shall I wear?

Just there commenced the *pas de deux* that
partnered me
with *What I Really Am*, despite the battering
I daily took from *Please Approve Of Me*.
And whether love depended on
plot or scenery,
gender, nation, colour, class, society,
or simply chattering,
one of me dressed to pacify the audience,
while the other, under my skin,
kept faith within.

Till fashion whispered, 'All you need, dear,
is a naked self.
Stress-free, perfect for summer or winter wear,
stretchable outside and in,
cheap, chic, dependable, off the shelf.'
So out I went and bought the latest thing in skin,
sexy as sin.
Since when (shocking the panicky crowd
that can't tell them apart)
skin wearing skin has been allowed
outside of Art.

Cashpoint Charlie

My office, my crouch, is by the Piccadilly cashpoint where
Clients of the Hong Kong and Shanghai Banking Co.
Facilitate my study of legs as they ebb and flow;
Legs, and the influence of sex and wealth on footware.

The human foot – wedge-shaped, a mini torso –
Used to be, like the monkey's, toed for zipping
Fast through jungles. Just how prehensile gripping
Got to be a closed shop for hands I'll never know.

Anyhow, feet are in jail now, shoes' prisoners,
Inviting comparison, ladies, with steel-tipped bullets,
And sadly, gentlemen, with coffins. My tiptop favourites
Are Dr Martens hammer-like hoofs and laceless trainers.

It's a proved fact that the shabbily shod give more.
Like knee-slashed jeans give more than knife-creased trousers.
And shivering junkies more than antique browsers.
What? Thanks to a glitch in the chem lab (not a war)

I'm legless. Or as good as…it all depends
On where you poke and what your count as me.
To "rise" I use a crutch. It helps the money,
And, like my filthy sleeping bag, offends

Your everyday dainty British git just bad enough
To make him pull his Balaclava face
Hard down over his sweet guilt. I make my case:
OK, if you hate me, you have to hate yourself,

And think it steady at him. Nothing's said, of course.
They never meet your eyes, not even the women
Yanking at their big-eyed kids like I was poison,
Then, with a tight look, opening their purse.

It's crazy, but I love them… it …taking the piss.
If that old guy, that Greek philosopher in his barrel,
Could see me now, in my sleeping bag, beside a hole
In a wall that spits out money, he'd be envious.

A Hot Night in New York

Midnight air's unbreathing steam
Shifts, with a sound of whips, to rain
As diamond-studded traffic meets
Its image doubled in the streets.

Shissssh as meteors plunge and spray.
Crescendo, now glissando, they
Cool and evolve a deeper night
From sibilant liquorice and light.

New York Is Crying

New York is crying. I didn't hear screaming, just dead, dark silence.
TYRONE DUX, New York policeman, quoted in
The Observer (London), 16 September 2001

Halfmast New York is crying for her children.
Her firemen, her policemen, her bagwomen,
Her smart investment analysts, her crooks,
Her execuwives in Gucci scarves and pantsuits,
Her TV chatterers and glossy-skinned presenters,
Her cleaners, waitresses and fast food cooks,
Her manicured secretaries and stubby-fingered punters,
Crying because they didn't die or scream.

Her preachers, her evangelists, her health cranks,
Her good-time girls and crack-addicts, her muggers,
Her Italian-Irish-Jewish politicians,
Her lawyers, paralegals and illegals,
Her internet whiz-kids and computer freaks,
Her trouble-shooters, paranoids, beauticians,
Deli proprietors, winos, hot musicians,
Dames with purple hair and crimson poodles...
Listen to them crying, but not screaming.

Is that Walt Whitman? Yes, but he is crying.
Hart Crane, in tears, is haunting Brooklyn Bridge.
Wystan, Dr Williams, mr cummings,
Miss Moore, Miss Bishop, look, they have come flying
In clouds of etymology, but crying.
Even John Astor and Henry Frick are trying,
Under the brassy marble of their monuments,
To sympathise with people who are dying.
Old Teddy Roosevelt, high on your moral horse,
What bracing words can dignify such crying?

But now a Mayor with a bedside manner,
And now a President in shining armour
Weep in the lens light of a billion eyes.
They want the world to notice they are crying.
Tears shall be sown in steel like dragon's teeth.
A crop of planes will pulverise the skies
While terrorists in terror cringe beneath.
Downtown, the bagel man on Chambers Street
Plasters his cart with frantic stars and stripes.
One wild-eyed Rasta with a bongo beats
Implacable voodoos under pulsing lights.
Flowers in the chainlink barrier are dying.

The ghostdust sours and settles with its smell
Of sulphurous flesh, stench of a Polish pit
Old Zbigniew Mirsky, eighty, knows too well;
One sniff, and his tower of hope falls into it.
The architect, America, was lying.
And here's the paper shop of Nizam Din
Locked behind shattered glass. No one's buying
His colourful books or letting strangers in.
The hole in New York is a hole in a belief
That desperately needs to hide itself in grief...
Professor X is lecturing, not crying.
Now, desert scenes and bursts of golden fire.
Those ragged children scuttling here and there
Are very small and far away, but crying.

A Cradle of Fist

'Solidity is a shifting desert,
air is energy,
as the world's clock watches
with its glass eye, *me*,
ticking the tempo of my pulse.

Almighty Word,
allow me to locate myself
in your cradle of fist.
Appoint me first
among the righteous.

Uproot what in me is
unblessed, bestial, sexed,
and let holiness
purge my spirit
of women and weakness.

I would, in the cockpit
of your purpose
be Azrael's talon
plundering, laying waste
the viper's nest.

Send me the clean veil
of the faceless
that I may kill
without conscience the featureless,
eyeless unfaithful.

And when I live again,
golden in the flower
of your will,
reveal to my mother
the face that is mine in Heaven.'

Clovenhoof's-bane

Nucleic crystals, pursed in the invisible,
Drift between pyres through pastures emptied of stock.
If myths were mortal, panic would cull the devil.
The season's immersed in slaughter and roiled muck.
What's learned how to fly, propagate, strike
                and hoard its luck?

Herd's-bane, heart's-bane, clovenhoof's-bane,
Wandering to and fro among the animals,
Choosing – to stoke its fires – the human brain
So that Virus the Small at last shall inherit the earth,
Outlasting love, the ordeal of it, grief,
              and the love of gain.

The Mass, The Media, The Market

The Mass

The Hydra in his ruff of heads
        would not have believed it –
each of my necks is attached
        to a different name.
Our appearance as one is achieved
        through tensions between us,
a balance of tentacles
        touching the green of this earth.
Great appetite and suction
        contract us advancingly together.
Why should we war?
        We are one growth.
What I consume, you shall consume.
        More must never be enough.

The Media

The descent into Hades
        will cost you three senses.
Take off your touch, please,
        your noses and mouths,
you won't be needing those.
        Eyes, though, and ears,
with their nerves,
        you may preserve.
Shall I inflate them for you?

You'll find it smoother, really,
        if you just let your bodies
drop off casually. There!
        Didn't I tell you?
Your heads will hold you up.

See how nice it is,
     floating in the other life?
You can fly to the past
     or visit the future,
switch on a lover,
     a lecture, a murder. It's
all guaranteed! You can suffer
     without pain,
score with the mighty, hear
     the gods speak.
Why ever go back to the
     feeble squalor of bodies?
So little is possible where
     everything's real.

The Market

I am your host.
     Why not call me
Midas? I rule because
     you make the rules.
Your health means
     my growth, so I
do what you say.

Watching you
     crawl for miles
towards my organ-
     isation, I offer you
my mouth,
     my resplendent intestine.
You feed me
     your time, your properties,
your investments.

It's in your interest
        I've swollen
to this size.
        Though you need me,
be careful, do please
        be careful.
I'm hungrier than my
        billions of
ingesters suggest. I'm
        the real
mercurial stomach
        of the world.
I turn flesh into cash.

A Report from the Border

Wars in peacetime don't behave like wars.
So loving they are.
Kissed on both cheeks, silk-lined ambassadors
Pose and confer.

Unbuckle your envy, drop it there by the door.
We will settle,
We will settle without blows or bullets
The unequal score.

In nature, havenots have to be many
And havelots few.
Making money out of making money
Helps us help you.

This from the party of useful words. From the other,
Hunger's stare,
Drowned crops, charred hopes, fear, stupor, prayer
And literature.

Branch Line

The train is two cars linking
Lincoln and Market Rasen.

Late May. Proof everywhere from
smudged sunny windows
that the European Union
is paying the farmers for rape.

How unembarrassed they are,
wanton patches the colour of heat
dropped like cheap tropical skirts
on the proper wolds.

The trees have almost completely
put on their clothes.
They sway in green crinolines,
new cool generous Eves.

The hawthorn-snow
looks predictably cold, unclenching.

As the train parts green field from gold
a spray of peewits fans up in a bow wave.

Is that a new factory out there
where the sea might be?
A lighthouse? A tall methane candle,
lethal if it were to go out?

The train slowly judders and halts
for no visible reason.

Rooks squabble in a maple.
A blackbird ferries an enormous worm to a nest.
Staring cows bend again to their munching.

Meaningless life, I'm reading in the TLS,
a nexus of competing purposes...

God is impossible.

Life is impossible.

But here it is.

A Tourists' Guide to the Fens

Level Cambridgshire, islands
of England
apportioned by drain and motorway;

dolls-house villages that have lost
their childhood;
roses called *peace* and *blessing*

exclusive to frilly white cottages
under pie-crust thatch.

Can you hear it?
The wind? Or traffic?

The low-hummed roar of saurian lorries
and a soughing avenue of 18th-century limes
sound the same.

In another film,
the heroine escapes with the hero
into rural Cambridgeshire *circa* 1666...

A field of barley, feathered;
a fen full of sky-blue butterfly flax,
undulations like the ocean's

rolling right up to the cameraman's
pollen-dusted loafers.
And when Anthea sets up her easel

to catch in watercolour
a picturesque angle of the almshouses,
she scrupulously omits

electrical wiring and TV paraphernalia
that, in strange time, connect her to

'the brutish, uncivilised tempers of these parts'...
the cottagers' corpses stinking,
unburied by the furrows,

Christ's men in retreat
at the Fever House at Malton, 'there

to tarry in time of contagious
sickness at Cambridge
and exercise their learning and studies

until such time
as God pleased to make the city
safe again for commerce and superior minds'.

Carol of the Birds

Feet that could be clawed, but are not...
Arms that might have flown, but did not...
No one said, 'Let there be angels!' but the birds

Whose choirs fling alleluias over the sea,
Herring gulls, black backs carolling raucously
While cormorants dry their wings on a rocky stable.

Plovers that stoop to sancify the land
And scoop small, roundy mangers in the sand,
Swaddle a saviour each in a speckled shell.

A chaffinchy fife unreeling in the marsh
Accompanies the tune a solo thrush
Half sings, half talks in riffs of wordless words,

As hymns flare up from tiny muscled throats,
Robins and hidden wrens whose shiny notes
Tinsel the precincts of the winter sun.

What loftier organ than these pipes of beech,
Pillars resounding with the jackdaws' speech,
And poplars swayed with light like shaken bells?

Wings that could be hands, but are not...
Cries that might be pleas yet cannot
Question or disinvent the stalker's gun,

Be your own hammerbeam angels of the air
Before in the maze of space, you disappear,
Stilled by our dazzling anthrocentric mills.

To Phoebe

(at five months)

How in this mindless whirl of time and space
Find words to welcome one small human child?
Shakespeare was lucky, art wore Shakespeare's face
And nature kept the virtues neatly filed.
God's earth was fixed, and round it ran the sun,
A temperamental lantern on a skate.
Our lives by stars were wound up or begun;
The universe was Heaven's unspoiled estate.

But now, lost to the angels, it appears
We share with rats and fleas a murky source.
Our plaited genes mean nothing to the spheres;
Contingency, not prayer, will plot your course.

Yet no small Phoebe *circa* sixteen-three
Was ever free to be what you shall be.

Almost Lives

(Two Twentieth Century Gentlemen)

I

Despite the sharp, perforated edges of its calendars,
        time doesn't tear off cleanly.
Roses of it still twine freshly behind the sporting posters
        tacked to his bedroom wall –
Maurice's. Rugby to Cambridge to India, tipped to succeed,
        fever-dead at twenty.
Yet, here he is, winning the Hundred Metres. That must be
        a King's May Ball.
Does the dance music trapped in those stacked 78s
        ache to be played?
Smile at the haircuts, blow dust off the foxtrots.
        Clever, smooth-headed Maurice
Who might have scratched history, whose unreplayable dates
        replay him for us
Stereotyped, the Oxbridge colonial nabob (n.b. Jewish)
        he never became.
Massacre, muddle, retreat, then exit the Empire.
        Maurice not even to blame.

II

Then there was Len, born 1901, whose luck stopped ticking
        on the dot of his top hat
When emboldened by Tattinger (cousin Aggie's wedding)
        he fingered his collar
Breathing 'hope for the future' to an ear's nest of auburn hair.
        Crossly she whispered, 'Stop that!'
Later, outblushing the camelias, helplessly he heard,
        'Him? I'd sooner marry a wombat!'
Once was enough. Retreating, poisoned by women
        but unfazed by bombs, he secured
Himself in Economic Warfare, riddling while London
        burned, a whizz at the crossword.
Then, with his books and manservant, he retired to a time
        that never happened after 1949.
And staled there fifty years. To grey working nieces, Uncle –
        his pipe, his stick, his hearing aid
That toiled through breakfast whistling like a kettle –
        left half a million when he, gently, died.

Questionable

When she laid a light hand on his elbow saying
'I seem to be hungry,' she knew she meant
Oh, to be thirty years younger,
lying with his head in my lap
tracing with one feather finger
the beautiful bowline of his upper lip.

But when he replied in his charming accent,
'Let's go find something to eat,' it wasn't evident –
no? – he meant more than that.
So Nudeln mit Pfifferling had to do.
Maybe what his eyes said was innocent.
Maybe it was not. She never knew.

In Passing

Suppose I had paused a few seconds
clattering down those public stairs,
and you (by chance?) had met me.
Would a look or a brush of hands have swept away
or thickened the cloud between us?

Say I had found you on the phone
and not clicked off so quickly.
Would you have heard the heartdrum
beating, beating where my tongue should be?
Nothing's happened; nothing's to confess.

You asked how experience becomes a poem
in the weightless hour that makes poetry.
Look, it's happening now in a country,
not home, not foreign,
in language that puts its clothes on carefully

after unpaid, love-making labour in that
dark, erotic mill, the imagination.
Imagine believing that a cloud can be
talked into becoming a mountain long after
it has lost itself in common day.

Prophylactic Sonnets

I

Eyes fall in love before their users dare
Measure the turbulence behind their gaze,
So, without speech or touch, deep looks lay bare
The underside of smooth, well-mannered ways.
In love, this is the transcendental stage
That if prolonged would sweeten all our lives,
No groans, no grapplings, no hormonal rage,
An end to faking husbands and false wives.
For looks subsist on wish-fulfilling dreams
While firm interpretations wait in doubt.
No shared desire is carried to extremes
When neither cares to say what it's about.
Unless those looks were really saying this:
Love flies in safety over time's abyss.

II

If I'm your book and you have found the page
Where, in the epic, randomly we met
In canto sixty-eight (that was my age),
Now look between us at the alphabet:
You at the *m* or *n* of your career,
Hacking, bewildered, through the savage wood,
I at my *x y z*, yet in the clear,
And primed to be your Beatrice if I could.
There to your left, my pages pile asleep
In brutal certainty of what has been,
While on your right, no ploy of plot will keep
That too determined end from looking thin.
When there's no more to read, I think you'll see
How well you knew my book, how little me.

43

III

O Übermenschen, flex your miracles!
Nature complies but science overcomes.
So greed's technology shows off its skills,
October strawberries and April plums.
Nothing is fixed that won't defer to power.
The planet, oyster-sized and up for sale,
Auctions its primal assets by the hour,
Then fights for cash by electronic mail.
Fame's not reliable, no more is sex.
Women can mate or unmate at a whim,
Yet choose their offspring's genome, pick 'n' mix,
Or make a him of her, a her of him.
Consider, too, this miracle of mine:
Verse conquers love, ten syllables a line.

The Inn
(for Peter)

It appeared to be an inn for actors, so our boss
Asked for a room with four beds. The landlady,
Quaint in a lace mobcap, shook her lustrous
Green ribbons at his trilby hat. Only three
Beds were free, the fourth was let to her lover.
My sister and I were laying our charms in rows
On our childhood bed when into that oak-ribbed chamber
Burst the lovers in eighteenth-century clothes,
Her furbelows fish scales against his velvet pelt.
Hearing their pantings and bird-like cries, I knew
If I looked too closely they would turn to dust.
As I would, dreaming, if I couldn't reach you,
Solid, asleep in this inn we've carefully built
Of seasoned faith and uncorrupted trust.

Some Poems from Cwm Nantcol

The Wind, the Sun and the Moon

For weeks the wind has been talking to us,
Swearing, imploring, singing like a person.
Not a person, more the noise a being might make
Searching for a body and a name. The sun
In its polished aurora rises late, then dazzles
Our eyes and days, pacing a bronze horizon
To a mauve bed in the sea. Light kindles the hills,
Though in the long shadow of Moelfre, winter
Won't unshackle the dead house by the marsh.
Putting these words on paper after sunset
Alters the length and asperity of night.
By the fire, when the wind pauses, little is said.
Every phrase we unfold stands upright. Outside,
The visible cold, the therapy of moonlight.

The Unaccommodated

Like winter in the hills, the heft of their
lingering, still unburied shadows
in the wind's hoarse uprush
out of heaps of rock they lived in.
      Millennia later,
houses rise stone by stone, neighbour
by aching neighbour; impenitent webs of wall
      from the haunted spills.

Sickness in the dark they lived in.
Candlelight hoarding sweet secrets
      in the mice's corners.
Girls giving birth by rushlight.
The same fires set by the dead
in a theatre of cheekbones and foreheads;
a hand through the night, stitching cloth
      with a stiff thread.

Just as constant, the cold they lived in,
each minute paid down on an open Bible
      one by one by one
in hard brass grudged by the pendulum.
Firelight is the lurch of a hummed,
      lambent, discontinuous meditation,
nimbus of their voices and table talk.
Flick off the mains and you'll be them.

Under Moelfre

A poem for a marriage

Whatever it is we share with folds of rock
Is nowhere to own and doesn't own a name.
Its hug was ours before we learned to talk.
When we stop speaking, it will be the same,
For all our anxious bustling and assessing.

Sense says there's only us, the way we dither
Plan, write poems, seriously discuss.
When man and woman come to live together,
Why invoke the presence of a place?
Unless the place, responsive to hard pressing,

Carries in ice age crevices some spoor,
Some truth the planet cherishes, or seed,
That finds a future in the years before.
Deep age in rock, like weather, meets our need
And blesses when it doesn't know it's blessing.

Why Take Against Mythology (1)

That twilight skyline, for example,
the more I look at it,
the more I see a skull
crushed into the hill, nose
chipped flat, jaw
thrust up, full bush of
genitals stirring just
in the right place.

See him? No, stand
here, clear of the house.
Uncork a magnum
of imagination, man!
Inflame your heart
with my enchanted giant.
Figure his resurrection
in your dreams, or art,

But make him art, not fact.
For when daylight comes back
it will tear him apart.
And how could I love,
dear, a Wales
made of ice-cut rock? No tales
in the making of mountains,
no mind in the dark?

Why Take Against Mythology (2)

Why, love, do you persist
in personifying natural events?
That's not imagination, it's arrogance,
locating fate in stars, off-loading
guilt on rocks that were liquid once
eons before our first
purposeless cells
commenced their crawl.

You like to imagine?
Imagine nuclei moiling themselves
alive in steamy crevices,
continents travelling and clashing.
Then, three miles high, a grinding
plain of ice, a Pleistocene caul,
gouging, sculpting, furrowing
this scoop of valley.

Before art, lichens delicately
etched that cliff-face.
Millions of millennia formed
bracken, heather, gorse.
Facts? They'll be minted by imagination
once daft mankind
stops conjuring out of mass and force
false spirit-shadows of his own mind.

Attacking the Waterfall
(North Wales)

Curlews long gone from the valley,
and now swallows that used to swoop
and then again swoop,
lightening the load of the sky,
are this summer so few
that the thrill of their sighting,
just one? no, two, is a flicker of hope,
a flare marginal to their dying –
though the rhaeadr still quarrels intimately
with its mountains,
skirmishing, water against water, quick time,
slow time with the sloth of stones.

As a hemisphere skews towards the sun,
the cwm competes, clock time, against migrants
raring to have fun.
Up, counter to the cataract, they swarm,
warrior ants in wetsuits and cocky helmets,
gutsy, braggish, betting on their luck,
pitching their rise against a fall mad Adam
fancied was his own.
For sure, the fall is nature's.
Listen! The old man's raging on. *Shit! Fuck!*
ricochet from the battleground – gunshot,
or a fighter plane, maybe, testing the barriers.

Spring Poem

(for John Heath-Stubbs)

Language raked tribute from her screen all winter,
but now comes a day in spring when restless Eve
runs out of words to commit to her lord computer
and in neglect of her career, plays diligently
and with delight on the vacuum cleaner:

Let Cambria vouchsafe to her hard unloving hills
a sharp green glance of enchantment.
Let daffodils be scrubbed until they shine.
Let windows crack open and kick back the April sun.

Let be, let be, too eloquent Eve.
Give up newfangledness for nourishment.

Without Me

A north wind light this morning,
Who will watch it
gilding the hennas of the marsh?
Between the iron gate's upright
and its top rung
death's in her diamond collar.
And if ewes last night
laid glistening pebbles, the pasture
will be pointillist with dung,
with burnished dung-flies busily feeding.

After heavy rain, a flood of sun,
but not for me the rainbows hanging
one   one   one
from tearful lines of crooked fencing
that will rust by noon.
Now, what's that shadow by the pigsty
pecking, looking, pecking?
Fly away, silly bird, fly!
Whose pasture will be grazing
on your white bones soon?

May Bluebells, Coed Aber Artro

No Greek self-pitying hetairos in blue-rinse curls,
        the north's true Hyacinthus non-scriptus
(much written about, nonetheless),
        beloved of Hopkins, who in Hodder Wood
perfectly caught its 'level shire of colour'
        while his companions talked.

West Country 'Crowfoot' or 'Grammer Graegles',
        in Welsh translated 'Cookoo's Boot',
'Blue of the Wood', 'Welcome Summer',
        each silky delicate bell-stalk
carrying its carillon to one side,
        dusky wine-cups, ringers of creamy anthers,
in Cymbeline misnamed 'the azured harebell'
        by Arviragus...

And even in our time,
        self-assigned to resurrection.
Camping gas set burning
        at the lowest visible flame.
Ice-age giant still nourishing
        the trodden mulch and green enchantment
of his daughter beechwood, watering
        one more summer out of hazy veins.

Green Mountain, Black Mountain

I

White pine, sifter of sunlight,
Wintering host in New England woods.
Cold scent, icicle to the nostril,
Path without echo, unmarked page.

    I formed you, you forgot me,
    I keep you like a fossil.
    The air is full of footprints.
    Rings of the sycamore spell you.
    Your name spills out on April ground
        with October leafmould...

Beech bole, cheekbone of the interior,
Sugaring maple, tap of sour soil.
Woody sweetness, wine of the honeybark,
Mountain trickle, bitter to the tongue.

    You acquired me out of wilderness,
    Grey maples streaked with birches,
    With your black-shuttered
    White wooden houses flanked with porches,
    Your black-painted peeling front doors.

Pairs of shuttered windows,
Sheltered lives.
Child's work, the symmetry,
Thin graves for narrow souls.

    Terra there was before *Terra Nova*.
    You brought to my furred hills
    Axes, steeples; your race split
    Hugely on the heave of the Atlantic...

In April the earth serves patiently its purpose.
Trees unclench their closed crimson fists against return.
How many weeks before ease will annul these
Dark, matted, snow-beaten scraps of mowin?

Dry wind-eaten beechleaves
Flutter under their birth arch.
Steeplebush and blackberry
Stoop to beginnings.

Green mountain with its shadow future,
Unwritten days in the buried stone.
Black mountain, colour of roots,
Clay in the roof, gag to the mouth.

II

In Border Powys, a Land Rover
stalls on a hill track.
Dai Morgan climbs out with a halter,
plods to a sodden field where
a mare and her colt have mauled
the wet soil of Welsh weather
all a mud-lashed winter.

Unlatching the gate, he
forces the halter on the caked,
anxious head of the mare,
then leads her away to where
a plan of his own makes fast
to some spindle purpose
the fate of the three of them.

The inscrutable movements of the man
puzzle the horses, who
follow him, nevertheless,
up the piebald track,
snowdeep in drift in places,
tyre-churned with red mud.

These are the Black Mountains
where the drenched sleep of Wales
troubles King Arthur in his cave,
where invisible hankerings of the dead
trouble the farms spilled over them –
the heaped fields, graves and tales.

And Dai, with his brace of horses,
nervous of strangers, inbreeder of races,
is Teyrnon still, or Pryderi the colt-child,
fixed without shape or time
between the ghost-pull of Annwfn,
that other world, underworld, feathering
green Wales in its word-mist,
and the animal pull of his green dunged boots.

III

Rain in the wind
    and the green need of again
        opening in this Welsh wood.

'Vermont' I want to call it.
    Green Mountain, rafter
        over sleepers in the black

hill of returnings, shadows
    in the dry cave
        of the happened.

At peal of memory
    they rise in tatters, imperative
        the word fossils,

webs of thready handwriting,
    typewritten strata, uncut stones
        culled for the typesetters' cemeteries

*

If you, mother, had survived
    you would have written...?
        As when we were children

and everything was going on
    forever in New Haven,
        you scratched in your journal,

It is a strange reaction but suddenly the war
has made it imperative to spend time at home
reading and being with my children.

The pen drew its meaning
    through vacancy,
        threading a history.

*

So what shall I do
    with this touchable page that has
        closed over doubt in her voice these forty years?

I set the words up on the table,
    feeling for continuities,
        tap them with my quick nail. Listen.

But her shell has buried her echo in them.
    It is small, hard, a milk tooth
        a guilt pebble, time preserved like an ammonite.

Then maybe on the second
    or the third day of March
        you overhear a blackbird in a dead elm,

or a thrush singing almost before you wake,
    or you walk unexpectedly into the calm
        ravage of a riverbank

where a broken branch
    kneels into rising water to remake
        predictable green tips,

and I know that it matters
    and does not matter...
        It is you in me who lives these things.

*

We thought she'd want us, knowing it was cancer,
But when we went to her she winced.
Her hand became a supplicating blur
That winter, and we didn't see her much.
There was a kind of wilting away in her
As if she couldn't bear the human touch
Of voices. Or it was something more
Unkind in us... resentful helplessness,
A guilty anger. She was dying
At us.   Dying was accusing.

IV

After April snow, such a green thaw.
A chiff-chaff chips a warmer home in that cloud-cliff.
The river bulges, flexing brown Japanese muscles,
moving its smooth planes in multitudes.
Threads of white melt stitch
the slashed flanks of the hill fields.

Soon the animal will be well again,
hunting and breeding in grass-covered bones.
It peers from these clinical windows,
apprehensive but healing.
To be whole will be enough.
To be whole and well and warm,
content with a kill.

V

Crossing the Atlantic. That child-pure
        impulse of away, retreating
                to our God-forgetting present

from the God-rot of old Boston and Leyden.
        To remove to some other place
                for sundry weighty and solid reasons.

And then to be the letter of the place,
        the page of the Lord's approval,
                within the raw green misery of the risk.

For there they should be liable to
famine and nakedness
and the want, in a manner, of all things.

Without things, then, the thing was to be done,
    the mountain renamed, the chance
        regiven. Taken again.

*

Crossing the Atlantic, Passport,
    briefcase, two trays of cellophane food
        and a B grade film.

No, I mean
    across to the America
        that lives in the film of my mind.

You would have to be
    alive there, reeled out
        from the spool of your life.

Not as a photograph,
    unhappiness or happiness staring
        from the onceness of a time,

but as the living practice of a now
    rehearsed as certain habits and expressions:
        your shoulders' loosened stoop to the piano,

the length of you decanted on a chair,
    animate in argument, ash scattered
        from your cigarette like punctuation.

And there, among the muses of your house,
    a breeding pack of violins, and cellos
        punished in the corners,

gleaming with the naked backs of girls
    smug in the enslavement of one lover
        or another since the eighteenth-century

made its music bread and solace
        for the likes of us who,
                having no other faith,

still kept our convenant with
        German Bach, with Schubert,
                after-dinner Mozart string quartets.

*

The Polish ghettos drained
        into the cattle cars.
                Murdered Vienna bled us violins.

*

Chestnut blossom with its crimson stigmata,
Stamen-thrust from confused hands,
Five white petals, multiple in competing order
So that each candlelabrum stands
As a tree of defeats around a *pietà*.

To be as one mother in a storm of sons,
The charred faces and cracked skulls of a
Comfortable century. Petal-white sands
Made of tiny shellfish. The crashed motorcycle
Where the sea withdraws with no grief at all.

VI

In dread of the black mountain,
Gratitude for the green mountain.
In dread of the green mountain,
Gratitude for the black mountain.

In dread of the fallen lintel and the ghosted hearth,
        gratitude for the green mountain.
In dread of the crying missile and the jet's chalk,
        gratitude for the black mountain.

In dread of the titled thief, thigh-deep in his name,
>gratitude for the green mountain.
In dread of the neon street to the armed moon,
>gratitude for the black mountain.

In dread of the gilded Bible and the rod-cut hand,
>gratitude for the green mountain.
In dread of the falling towers behind the blazing man,
>gratitude for the black mountain.

In dread of my shadow on the Green Mountain,
Gratitude for this April of the Black Mountain,
As the grass fountains out of its packed roots
And a thrush repeats the repertoire of his threats:

>*I hate it, I hate it, I hate it.*
>>*Go away. Go away.*
>*I will not, I will not, I will not.*
>>*Come again. Come again.*

Swifts twist on the syllables of the wind currents.

Blackbirds are the cellos of the deep farms.

Mowin (57) is the Vermonters' term for a hayfield or mowing field.

King Arthur in his cave (58) refers to the Welsh legend regarding Arthur and his warriors who are said not to be dead but asleep in a cave (sometimes Craig-y-Ddinas near Carmarthen). At the peal of a bell they will rise to rescue Wales from her oppressors when her need is greatest. Teyrnon and Pryderi are characters associated with horses in the First Branch of the *Mabinogion*. Annwyfn or Annwn is the Welsh otherworld, comparable to the Irish Sidh. The colours of things and creatures belonging to Annwfn are red and white.

The quotations in V are from William Bradford's *History of Plymouth Plantation* as quoted in Perry Miller's *The American Puritans* (New York, 1956).